JOHN WIL1
BARON WILLIAMS OF THAME
1500 – 1559

Michael J. Beech

Visit us online at www.authorsonline.co.uk

An Authors OnLine Book

Text Copyright © Michael J. Beech 2008

Cover design by Michael J. Beech and James Fitt ©

All rights reserved. No part of this publication may be reproduced, stored in a retrieval system, or transmitted in any form or by any means, electronic, mechanical, photocopy, recording or otherwise, without prior written permission of the copyright owner. Nor can it be circulated in any form of binding or cover other than that in which it is published and without similar condition including this condition being imposed on a subsequent purchaser.

ISBN 978-07552-0429-8

Authors OnLine Ltd
19 The Cinques
Gamlingay, Sandy
Bedfordshire SG19 3NU
England

This book is also available in e-book format, details of which are available at www.authorsonline.co.uk

JOHN WILLIAMS

BARON WILLIAMS OF THAME

1500 – 1559

FOUNDER OF LORD WILLIAMS'S SCHOOL THAME

In commemoration of the 450th anniversary of the foundation of the school
1559 – 2009

Dedicated to the memory of
John Fulkes
colleague and friend
whose life was so very much
associated with
Lord Williams's School

Rosencrantz: Take you me for a sponge, my lord?
Hamlet: Ay, Sir; that's soaks up the king's countenance, his rewards, his authorities. But such officers do the king's best service in the end; he keeps them, like an ape, in the corner of his jaw; ... when he needs what you have gleaned, it is but squeeze you, and, sponge, you shall be dry again.

Hamlet, Act IV, Scene II.

THE LIFE OF JOHN WILLIAMS 1500 – 1559
FOUNDER OF LORD WILLIAMS'S SCHOOL THAME

CONTENTS

Author's note
Introduction — John Williams and the national situation in mid-Tudor times

Chapter I	Early Life 1500 – 1536
Chapter II	Dissolution of the Monasteries 1536 – 1540
Chapter III	Treasurer of the Court of Augmentations 1544 – 1554
Chapter IV	Reign of Edward VI 1547 – 1553
Chapter V	The Rebellion of 1549
Chapter VI	Queen Mary's Reign 1553 – 1558
Chapter VII	The Burning of the Bishops
Chapter VIII	Lord Williams's Wealth
Chapter IX	The Final Year 1558 – 1559
Chapter X	Assessment of the Life of John Williams

Date list

Illustrations:

1. (page xii) John Williams – from his tomb in St Mary's Church, Thame
2. (page 35) Lord Williams presides over the burning of the two Bishops
3. (page 36) Lord Williams presides over the burning of Thomas Cranmer
4. (page 41) View of Rycote House
5. (page 46) School Statutes 1575 and John Williams's signature.
6. (page 51) Lord Williams and his first wife, St Mary's Church, Thame

AUTHOR'S NOTE

This account is based on research I did at the University of Warwick and in the Bodleian Library in 1989-90. It is intended to present a partial picture for the general reader of the life of Lord Williams, whose bequest provided for the founding of the present school at Thame which celebrates its 450th anniversary in 2009.

I write "a partial picture", because I have concentrated on events that centred on Thame and the surrounding area, but in the interest of clarity and context, I have also covered events in other parts of the country. There are such gaps in the sources that I could find very little or nothing about the man for long periods, and I found very little personal material written in his own hand. Those personal records which do exist are of a financial nature or are formal letters asking for, or granting favours.

In my introduction, I have taken on the responsibility of explaining the background events of the time and have interpreted Williams's actions accordingly. I have always kept in mind that he has to be judged against a very different set of circumstances from today. Even so, he emerges as an ambitious, sometimes ruthless man, even for his own time, whose corrupt activities attracted the attention of the Council on occasion. Yet he managed to survive in an age when one false move could mean ruin or death.

My sources are too numerous to detail here, but among the Primary Sources are the Letters and Papers of Henry VIII (London, 1892); the Calendars of State Papers Domestic and of Spain from 1547 to 1567; John Foxe's "Acts and Monuments" (Book of Martyrs) (London, 1583); "The Diary of Henry Machyn" (Camden Society n° XLII, London 1848). I also used Strypes "Annals", Vol. 1 (London, 1634), his "Memorials of Cranmer" (London, 1634) and F.G. Lee's "History of the Prebendal Church of the Blessed Virgin Mary of Thame" (London, 1883). More recent useful secondary works include A. Vere-Woodman's "The Bucks and Oxon Rising, 1549", Oxoniensia, Vol. XXII, and W.C. Richardson's "History of the Court of Augmentations", (Baton Rouge, 1961).

I have included exact dates where possible so as to bring out the complexity of events and the speed with which they could unfold. We must remember that communications were no faster than a galloping horse on land and an unwieldy sailing ship at sea, both of which were at the mercy of the weather, unreliable messengers and lurking enemies.

Where the reader can easily understand the original text (albeit with occasional odd spellings and abbreviations), I have deliberately left it as it was, to bring the period more to life. However, I have sometimes put extracts into modern prose and have so indicated.

All dates refer to the modern calendar, even though the New

Year did not begin until March in those days. Thus, February 1533 to us now was then February 1532.

Finally, I would again like to thank those many people who gave me much help in 1989 and 1990 including in particular Professor J. Scarisbrick of the University of Warwick and those who have supported me in producing this study, namely Aisling Begley, Graham Thomas and Stuart Davies of the OTA, David Wybron, Principal of LWS, close friends who offered welcome advice and of course, my dear wife, Marie-Claude, who taught French at LWS and who patiently typed out the original thesis and put this work onto the computer for me.

M. J. B. 2008

John Williams, Baron Williams of Thame

INTRODUCTION

Apart from historians and citizens of Thame, few today will have ever heard of John Williams, yet he was well known in his own time. He was always there on the edge of momentous political events, and sometimes at their centre. For example, he supervised the burning of two bishops, and later the ex-Archbishop of Canterbury. He was present at major royal events; he personally arrested the Protector Somerset and his last position was as President of the Council which governed Wales.

We have to marvel at a man who successfully managed to serve loyally four very different monarchs at a time of enormous political, religious and economic upheaval. That he survived is in itself remarkable, but that he was able to steadily increase his fortune until he was one of the richest men in England when he died, is even more so.

How was he able to cling on to his position? Was it because he was clever enough never to be caught on the wrong foot? Maybe because he does not seem to have pursued serious political ambitions or was it simply because he became a useful and experienced dogsbody at the disposal of the monarch? His ambitions seem only to have been limited to accumulating wealth and social status. Thus, he died in his bed, having moved in dangerous Court circles for over thirty years, during which time so many of his contemporaries died on the scaffold.

Although this account of John Williams is written in commemoration of his founding of the school, the reader may well be taken aback, if not shocked, by the story that lies behind the generous bequest made in his will. As already intimated, he acted somewhat like a 16th century Vicar of Bray who, like a weathercock, turned in the direction of whichever political wind happened to be blowing. To our eyes Williams may appear as a Machiavellian character with few scruples and no sense of Christian morality, but we must take into account that his world was very different (or was it?) from ours. It is against this background that we should judge him.

Let us imagine then an England which was hardly more removed from decades of civil war than we are from the Second World War, and those memories were still so intense as to inspire Shakespeare decades later. Imagine next, the later thirty years of Williams's life, corresponding to the time since Mrs Thatcher came to power in 1979, when four very different governments with near absolute power ruled England in the space of only twelve years; when four chief ministers of the Crown were beheaded, as were three members of the royal family – all queens; and an Archbishop of Canterbury and two other bishops were burnt alive in public within a day's walk of Thame. This was a time when nearly one third of the land of England which had belonged to the Church, was transferred into lay hands, when centuries of religious loyalties, practices and institutions were wilfully desecrated or destroyed in an era when nearly everyone believed in the existence of God and in his power to determine the course of one's life. A great number of newly enriched families profited from these momentous changes to rise up the social ladder, and among them of course, John Williams. They then took up positions of authority which would eventually determine the direction of events towards yet another Civil War, this time between Crown and Parliament.

All these developments were taking place against a background of previously unknown inflation (prices rose x 5 during the 16th century) and when the belief in the God-given "just price" for goods was undermined and eventually disappeared. Common land was being enclosed for the sole benefit of the large wool-producing sheep farmers who turned out tenants from their life-giving holdings to join the ranks of the unemployed. Such people had to turn to begging and thieving[*] to survive and were thus a constant threat to law and order which was largely maintained by Justices of the Peace like John Williams.

These officers were appointed by the Crown at a time when there was no organised police force or a standing army to keep control. Their interest lay in maintaining the social status quo and they were only too willing, even anxious to quell any signs of discontent, so thin was the layer of law and order spread over that society. We should also keep in mind the periodic bouts of plague

---

[*] Hence the nursery rhyme, "Hark, hark, the dogs do bark, the beggars are coming to town..."

and other epidemics and diseases among men and animals, spells of drought and flood and of crop failures which devastated the lives of hundreds of thousands of people when the total population of England and Wales is estimated to have been about 2 million.

Thus, Williams faced a dangerous, uncertain, everyday life and he would have been aware that if he and his family were to survive he would have to live according to a moral code very different from the ideal.

Unless he was particularly cynical, Williams would have seen God and the Devil at work behind the changes that were occurring during his life time. It would not have been difficult therefore, for him to persuade himself that it was his moral duty to offer his loyalty and resources to whomsoever God saw fit to grant power, so great was the need to maintain order and preserve stability. He could not see into the future, he had to live from day to day and if in the process others suffered, especially those seen as no longer favoured by God, then so be it!

At the end of his life he may have come to realise that his ultimate personal duty was to atone to God for any sins he had inadvertently committed in the course of a life that caused him to have to twist and turn in so many directions.

I leave you, the reader, to judge the man as you read the account which follows.

CHAPTER I
EARLY LIFE

John Williams was probably born in 1500 in Burghfield, Berkshire, but there is some doubt as to the exact year and it may have been as late as 1503. His father, Sir John Williams, a native of Glamorgan and a direct descendant of the last independent ruler of Wales, was the first of his family to anglicise his name. He had fought for Henry VII at the Battle of Bosworth, 1485, and so the family was already well placed for advancement under the Tudor monarchs when John was born. We know nothing about John's upbringing but can speculate that he had a tutor and probably spent some years in the household of some close friend or relative of his parents, learning the skills expected of a gentleman such as riding, hunting, archery and dancing before going on to train as a lawyer. At the same time, he was building up contacts in that relatively small social world which would serve him well in later life. It was as a consequence of such contacts that in 1524 he married Elizabeth Bledlowe, a rich widow from the Thame area. Not long afterwards, he purchased Rycote House, (now destroyed except for the Chapel) where his three sons and two daughters were born. It seems the house was modelled on a similar design to that of Hampton Court Palace, though much smaller, and it was surrounded by a moat.

In 1526, John was appointed as a Chancery official for Cardinal Wolsey, the effective ruler of England until 1529. The next year, he was granted a £10 patent to keep a greyhound for King Henry VIII. It is of interest here to note that Lord Williams's escutcheon is supported by a pair of greyhounds, constant reminders of how that lowly, but significant office became the base on which he was able to build his career at Court. It was perhaps through his distant kinship with Thomas Cromwell, the successor to Cardinal Wolsey as Chief Minister of the realm, that on 6 April 1530, he was appointed Clerk of the King's Jewels with a salary of 20 marks (1 mark = 2/3 of a £). Thus, he acquired experience in the administration of the royal finances and an influence at Court which he could not otherwise have gained because this office was within the royal household and therefore very close to the centre of government. After six years in the post, he was made joint Master of the King's Jewels with Thomas Cromwell and with whom he shared equally the annual fee of £50. From June 1540 when Cromwell was dismissed and later executed, John Williams became the sole Master of the King's Jewels until March 1544. During that period, he certainly made a considerable sum for himself, buying and selling royal jewels and plate. It has been calculated that he acquired £16,657 for himself, though this may be an exaggerated figure. Suspicions as to his honesty were first aroused when, on Christmas Eve 1541 at 7 o'clock in the evening, a great fire broke out in John's house at Elsingspital, London, during which "divers jewelles and goodes of the King's were embesylled and conveyed away". We can only conjecture who may have been responsible for the disappearance of such valuables! Certainly though, when a survey of the Royal Jewels was made in 1547, accusations were officially voiced about John Williams, but "he has not been charged because no survey has been made of the Jewels since the time of Thomas Cromwell".

However, the main route to fame and fortune began in 1536 when Thomas Cromwell appointed John Williams as one of five or six commissioners to look into the morals and financial affairs of the monasteries in England, an undertaking which gave him the opportunity to prove his loyalty to the Crown and also to profit from it. This revolutionary work fundamentally affected the whole history of England and is examined in some detail in the next chapter.

CHAPTER II
THE DISSOLUTION OF THE MONASTERIES

The closure across England and Wales of over eight hundred religious houses in the space of five years was an enormously important event which we today can hardly comprehend. The nearest we could conceive of such an event now would be for the State to forcibly take over eight hundred of the major companies in this country, dismiss most of the employees, pay the ex-directors a small pension and asset-strip the fabric merely to acquire the means to cope with an immediate financial crisis.

In spite of Henry's protestations to the contrary, the real motive was surely to grab easy money. He needed to counter the effects of inflation when his income was fixed, and to pay off debts accumulated by his very expensive foreign adventures, including wars against France, one of which was to result in the loss of the ship, The Mary Rose, on display in Portsmouth today. He also maintained a brilliant, but expensive Renaissance Court and was obliged to pay pensions and allowances to courtiers to keep them loyal to a king who had no permanent army or civil service outside the confines of the Court.

John Williams was one of those whose largely unpaid service was essential to the King. It was accepted therefore, that he profit from that service by rewarding himself out of commissions granted to him by the Crown and from the consequent powers of patronage which he wielded.

At first, Henry guided by Cromwell, was cautious in his attack on the monasteries. Arguing the dubious case that only the smaller houses were corrupt, irreligious, pro-papal institutions, he put pressure on the 1536 Parliament to legalise their closure. The monks were given the option of leaving religion or going into the larger monasteries.

The closing and stripping of the smaller monasteries contributed to a mighty rebellion in the north of England in 1536 (called The Pilgrimage of Grace) and which was only put down with difficulty by a fearful government. Once the rebellion was suppressed however, the government had gained enough confidence and experience to go for the larger monasteries. It was cunning enough to avoid a direct confrontation and so they were called upon to surrender voluntarily to Henry. It was made clear that their surrender would be seen as a sign of loyalty in view of their suspected continued loyalty to Rome. Furthermore, the extension of the Treason Laws by the King in Parliament put even more pressure on them to surrender.

What was an ambitious man like John Williams to do when faced with such a situation? He used his family links with Thomas

Cromwell to enrich himself and prove his loyalty to a king whose ruthlessness was becoming all too evident.

Early in 1535, Thomas Cromwell appointed a willing Williams to enquire into the state of the abbey lands in Oxfordshire. The latter next worked to organise the closure of the smaller monasteries in the county.

Then in 1538 we find Williams at work again, but this time his job was to bully the larger monasteries into surrendering to the King. As one of the five Commissioners appointed to cover the whole country, Williams was reporting to Cromwell in 1538 that he and his team had taken 5,000 marks of gold from Bury St Edmunds. He then went on to supervise the surrender of the great abbeys at Ely, Peterborough, Woburn, Reading, Winchester and Abingdon. At Abingdon, he stripped the abbey of its valuables between 7 and 11 March 1538 and left 100 barge loads of loot on the riverside to be shipped down the Thames to the royal treasury in London. Williams also closed several local abbeys. Studley, where the Abbess was Williams's sister, was closed on 19 November 1539. Eynsham was closed on 4 December, Notley, where there were thirteen monks in residence, on 9 December and there followed closures at Thame, Godstow, Wytham and Donnington.

Since we are all particularly concerned with Thame, I take the liberty of listing the valuables recorded at Thame Abbey during a government visitation led by Williams in 1537, prior to the intended closure.

9 chalices - 3 of silver gilt enamelled
- 6 of silver partly gilt

3 large solid altar crosses   - 1 of gold adorned with gems
                               - the others of silver encrusted with
                                 jewels
3 pastoral staves for the abbot - 1 of gold
                               - 1 of silver
                               - 2 of copper gilt [Dear Reader, do
                                 your sums!]
2 silver gilt censers and incense boats of the same metal
2 silver candlesticks for the high altar
1 pix of silver gilt
Other ornaments of inferior metal
38 sets of silk vestments
Hangings of silk, altar fronts, carpets, cushions, canopies, lecterns, prayer stools
In the refectory there were silver and silver gilt cups, plates, bowls, salt cellars and spoons.
(This was merely the treasure from Thame!)

As for the actual process of closure of an abbey, Williams has left us a detailed report to Cromwell when he went to Winchester on 21 September 1538. He describes all the treasures in the abbey, the co-operative and loyal nature of the Prior and the monks, and the taking down of the altar as follows:

(In modern English) "On going to our beds, we viewed the altar which we intend to take away with us. It will be worth dismantling but it will involve such work that it will take all Monday night and much of Tuesday morning. When this has been done, we intend to go to Hide and St Mary's to sweep away all the rotten bones which are said to be relics, so as not to be accused of only caring about the treasure and not bothering about the abomination of idolatry"!

It is to be noted how cynical a view Williams had of the task he was undertaking and that he thought it best to dismantle the altar at dead of night to avoid altercations with the local townsfolk until it was too late.

His undoubtedly diligent work was rewarded by being promoted to Treasurer of the Court of Augmentations on 31 March 1544. This Court had been set up in 1536 to receive, record and dispose of all the monastic property which came into the King's hands, and as we shall see, he made use of his position to enrich himself. In contrast to his work as Commissioner, it is less his diligence than his corruption and negligence which came to the fore in this next phase of his life.

CHAPTER III

TREASURER OF

AUGMENTATIONS 1544 – 1553

When he was appointed Treasurer of the Court of Augmentations, Sir John Williams became involved at last in the central affairs of state. By the end of the then financial year 1545 which was at Michaelmas, 29 September, Williams had learnt enough about the workings of the Court to be able to work there on his own. The revenues of Augmentations for that year were £32,739; they rose to £59,255 in 1546, but fell back to £48,303 in 1547. In that year the Court was amalgamated with that of General Surveyors, with Sir John in charge. In 1551, the total income of the two Courts was £159,195. Considering that the total revenue of the Crown in 1551 was £271,912, it is clear that Williams was heading the busiest and most important department of state and profiting from it. Thomas Pope who held the office up to 1540 died as one of the richest commoners in England, having taken over thirty manors for himself; yet his official salary was only £120 a year. Williams collected a salary of £300 plus fees for services and expenses and the right to retain his own chaplain.

Part of the reason why Williams made so much money for himself out of the Court of Augmentations is that once Henry died there was no longer that fear of the person of the monarch which had reined in previous office holders. Indeed, the two Protectors of the boy King Edward VI, the Dukes of Somerset and Northumberland, needed all the support they could get and were obliged to turn a blind eye on the activities of all except the most blatant of fortune seekers. An indication of the laxity of the times was that, between March 1544 and 1552, Williams never made a submission of his accounts to the auditors. When he was eventually obliged to present his accounts, he was subjected to several investigations, indicating that the authorities were quite sure that he was helping himself to more than was acceptable. On 26 October 1551, the Imperial Ambassador wrote to the Emperor Charles V, "In order to put the country's affairs in better shape, they [members of the Duke of Northumberland's party] have arrested a Mr [sic] John Williams, Treasurer of the Augmentations, who possesses a huge amount of livestock and is loathed by the people. Thus, they are trying to prove they mean to … ease the people's burdens". From this disinterested letter, we can see how Williams must have been a particular focal point for unrest during Edward's reign. The young king wrote in his journal that Williams had been arrested for paying out pensions to monks and chantry priests without first consulting the Council. At that time there was hardly any cash in the royal treasury and the Council wanted all payments postponed until the depleted reserves were refilled.

Williams was therefore summoned to appear before the Council at

7 o'clock on the morning of 3 April 1552 and he was sent to the Fleet Prison on 8 April with the proviso that no one was to converse with him. However, on 25 April the Council accepted that for his health's sake he should be allowed to walk in the gardens of the prison and to receive visits from his wife, children and friends. On 22 May, he apologised for not doing his duty properly and he was released provisionally after agreeing to pay the English ambassadors to Paris and Vienna the sums of £534 and £600 respectively – money that he had owed them for several months. On 2 June he was finally liberated and he resumed his office as Treasurer of Augmentations. Was this act of clemency because Williams was so useful to the government and, having given him a short, sharp shock, the Council was prepared to let the matter rest? Even so, the suspicions of corruption must have been a blow to his social standing and would no doubt have rankled with him. These concerns may help to explain why he had been willing to be the official who went to arrest Somerset at Windsor on 10 October 1549, and was later prepared to support Mary Tudor against Northumberland's attempt to put Lady Jane Grey on the throne in 1553.

Again, in 1554 during Mary's reign, the Council set up a commission of six men to look into the financial irregularities of Williams's work in the Court of Augmentations. It came to light that £31,226 in receipts from land sales by the Court had not been entered. Williams pleaded that negligence and carelessness on his part were responsible, and a large sum of money suddenly appeared in the accounts. In the accounts of May 1555, there is an item of £634 -19s - 0d paid by Williams towards the debt he had incurred while he was at the Augmentations office.

On 5 June 1556 he was again asked by the Council to explain a debt of £2,100 which he pledged to pay back by 20 June, but before then, the government pardoned all "debts, bonds, arrears, accounts and actions" against him. (We must here remember the role that Williams had played in ensuring Mary's succession in 1553 and that, only 3 months previously, he had supervised the burning of Cranmer without undue unrest).

Perhaps because of the suspicions surrounding the honesty of Williams, the government sent fewer and fewer warrants to the Court for payments and its business was allowed to decline until it was eventually incorporated into the Exchequer. When in January 1554, on the orders of Queen Mary, the Court stopped receiving revenues, it had become a much hated institution of government. A contemporary commentator, Henry Brinklow, talked of "the cruelties and suttylties of the Augmentations" and added, "a man were as good as to coming into the paynes of Hell as enter in to eyther of those ii courtys". [Augmentations and General Surveyors]. Other sources quote a prayer, "Christ, for thy bitter passion, save me from the Court of Augmentacyon". There were many other complaints against the officers of the Court who took every opportunity to wring fees, fines and other payments out of those called before it.

An American historian, W.C. Richardson, who in 1961 wrote a definitive history of the Court of Augmentations, commented on the compensation paid to Williams when the Court was dissolved that it was, "a travesty of justice considering the fact that he had defrauded the government of over £28,000 while in the Augmentations office".

CHAPTER IV

EDWARD VI 1547 – 1553

When Henry VIII died on the morning of 28 January 1547, aged 55 years and 7 months to the day, he was succeeded by his 9 year old son. Edward VI was an alert, well-educated boy who kept a useful daily journal of his life, but was too young to wield power even by the time he died at 16. Therefore Edward Seymour, brother of Henry VIII's third wife, Queen Jane (Seymour), Edward's mother, took control of his nephew and declared himself Lord Protector of England and Duke of Somerset. However, rival Court factions led by the Earl of Warwick which resented lands and honours being granted to the Protector's favourites, plotted against him and, in October 1549, they seized the Tower of London, still perceived as the seat of power in the realm. The Court retreated to Windsor, but there were not enough provisions laid in for any kind of resistance, so when Sir John Williams and two other commissioners arrived at the castle to arrest Somerset on seven charges of High Treason, most courtiers had already melted away and the arrest was easily made on 10 October. The next day, 500 horsemen arrived from London to conduct Somerset to the Tower where he was lodged.

Why Williams was entrusted to play such an instrumental role in the downfall of Somerset may be because he probably blamed Somerset's government for creating the situation whereby his estates in Thame and Rycote had been attacked in July 1549 by local inhabitants.

A near contemporary source reported that rioters from Oxfordshire and neighbouring counties "arose in great numbers and with great angre towards Sir John Willyams, disparked his park called Thame Park and kyllyd all ye deere; from thence they went to Rycote Parke and kylled all his deere, entered into ye place, and dranke theyr fyll of wyn, ale and beere, slew many shepe and ete them, with divers other myschives; from thens they went to Woodstock".

They were disgruntled at the way Williams had been enclosing common land for sheep farming and hunting. They had felt encouraged by a government commission of 1548 which had investigated breaches of the law concerning the arbitrary takeover of land held by commoners for several centuries and which had resulted in Somerset having issued controls to limit the spread of sheep farming.

All this helps explain why the Thame rioters not only killed Williams's sheep and deer but destroyed all the newly erected fences as well.

Another reason why Williams resented Somerset was a personal grievance which needs to be looked into. On 8 July 1547, the Crown under Somerset's control, had granted Thame Abbey and some of its land previously granted to Williams in 1542, to the Duke himself who now collected the rents due on that land.

Naturally, once Williams had arrested Somerset he expected to be rewarded by a grateful Council which now fell under the control of the Earl of Warwick who promptly proclaimed himself Duke of Northumberland in 1551. Thus, at the behest of Northumberland, Thame Abbey and its lands were officially handed back to Williams by Somerset shortly before the latter was executed.

CHAPTER V

THE 1549 REBELLION

Having explained the personal animosity of Williams towards Somerset prior to the 1549 troubles, we shall now examine how other factors of discontent in the Thame area had built up to explode into rebellion in the summer of 1549.

In 1530, Henry VIII had passed through Thame riding alongside Anne Boleyn, his mistress, and with Queen Catherine (of Aragon) riding behind them. The inhabitants of Thame "hung their heads" in disapproval, thus letting it be known that they were in sympathy with the Queen and the traditional order.

In 1537, the Vicar of Thame observed the feast day of St Thomas a Beckett (who was considered to have died a martyr, at the hands of Henry II's henchmen), saying "the people would have it so". On that same day, Richard Child, a townsman of Thame, learning that some men were working that day instead of treating it as a holy day, remarked that he wished their horses' necks were broken and their carts set on fire. For this remark, a government informer reported him as a supporter of the Northern Rebellion, known as the Pilgrimage of Grace, which in 1536, had created the greatest threat to royal authority in the whole of the sixteenth century. In 1541, when Henry again rode through Thame, rumours flew around the town that "the King would have the crosses and the jewels of the church" (St Mary's!).

All the events quoted above point to an assumption that the people of Thame, as far as we can tell, were conservative. They resented the religious changes involving the removal of all aspects of papal authority and which were destroying their traditional way of life. In particular, they had witnessed Williams personally supervising the closure of Thame Abbey and becoming ever richer on the proceeds of his despoiling activities all over the region. Their unease and suspicions increased when, in February 1549, Williams supervised an inventory of all church goods in Thame and in June, the first Book of Common Prayer in English replaced the Latin Mass Book or Missal.

It is therefore not surprising that when rebellions broke out across England from East Anglia to the West Country, severe action was taken by Williams and his peers to prevent the two arcs of rebellion joining together and threatening London. For two months the rebellion raged and Williams's estates suffered badly. The government tried to blame it on "sundery priests", but the reasons were far more complex.

Williams must have feared the complete breakdown of all law and order, only tenuously imposed half a century before, and always under threat. Thus on 19 July, Williams who was perceived as second only in status to a group of 18 shire gentry, joined Lord

Grey of Wilton with 1,500 soldiers to arrange for selective hangings from among two hundred prisoners taken from particularly rebellious parts of Oxfordshire. The heads of the rebels were then to be mounted in the highest place in their town, "for the more terror of the said evil people"! It was decided that two of the rioters should be hanged in Thame; surely an indication of the hatred that Williams had incurred and his own fear of possible consequences once Lord Grey had moved out of the county.

For lack of actual evidence that religious concerns were the basis of the hatred towards Williams, it could be concluded that, as far as the Thame area was concerned, the main worry of the common people was that they were being deprived of valuable pastureland by Williams. He set out not only to increase his wealth but also his social status by being able to boast of 2 deer parks, at a time when such recreation grounds were seen as a symbol of social privilege.

Weight can be added to the above argument when we note that a secondary leader of the Oxfordshire Rising was Thomas Bouldry, described as a wealthy yeoman who came from Great Haseley. This village lay within three miles of Thame and was an even shorter distance from Williams's estate at Rycote where his magnificent house and grounds reflected his newly acquired wealth.

Then, on 7 August 1549, Williams wrote to the Council in London that, "the Oxfordshire papists are at last reduced to order, many of them being apprehended and some gibbeted and their heads fastened to the walls." Among those hanged were a vicar from Banbury and the priests from Deddington, Islip, Watlington, Chipping Norton, Bloxham and others further afield.

Can we discern a note of vindictive satisfaction in Williams's report that law and order had been restored? His property and status had been threatened by those very tenants who surrounded him every day and, of course, his standing with the government depended on his successful quelling of the rebellion. The Duke of Somerset had described the risings as "a plague of fury among the vilest and worst sort of men" and the rebels as conceiving " a wonderful hatred against (all) gentlemen ... and taketh them all for their enemies".

CHAPTER VI
QUEEN MARY'S REIGN 1553 – 1558

When the 33-year-old Queen Mary succeeded her brother, Edward VI, the whole religious structure of the country and its politics changed. Mary was a devout Catholic, the grand-daughter of Ferdinand of Aragon and Isabella of Castile, the two most renowned Catholic monarchs, and cousin of the most powerful contemporary sovereign, the Holy Roman Emperor, Charles V. Her mother, Catherine of Aragon, had been the uncontested and popular Queen-consort of England for twenty years and then, from 1529, Mary had been forced to witness what was in her eyes, the illegal annulment of her mother's marriage to Henry, her own bastardisation and the wilful destruction of most aspects of the Catholic faith in England.

The cult of Protestantism which replaced it, denying Papal authority, the essentials of the Mass, the concept of Purgatory and all the earthly infrastructure associated with it – the monasteries, chantries, the role and status of the priest as intermediary between God and man, and the use of Latin - was a horrifying heresy and an anathema to her.

Immediately, she set about re-establishing the old rites and traditions as far as circumstances and limited resources would allow, not for the sake of merely saving her own soul, but for the salvation of the souls of her subjects as well. Once established, she decided on a political marriage to Prince Philip of Spain, son of Charles V, to promote the cause of European Catholicism and she embarked on a determined, political crusade to eliminate all those who were associated with Protestantism and who would not repent and return to the Catholic Church. The one significant exception was the ex-Archbishop of Canterbury, Thomas Cranmer, who had pushed through the annulment of her mother's marriage and had issued the protestant Book of Common Prayer in English. Cranmer had, under pressure, recanted but Mary was not prepared to let him escape the ultimate punishment.

It is against this background that we shall view the role of Sir John Williams in the controversial events with which he was associated in the next five years. We should remember that, in 1553, he was already viewed as a fickle individual in political circles and was clearly hated by the local populace. He therefore had to move quickly and decisively in order to establish good relations with the new queen.

On 6 July 1553, on the very day that Edward died, Sir John left London for Oxfordshire. He must have known that the protestant Duke of Northumberland would not easily yield to Mary and so, when on 10 July the Duke proclaimed his protestant daughter-in-law, Jane Grey, a great-niece of Henry VIII, Queen, Williams proclaimed Mary as Queen in Oxfordshire on 13 July. Quite apart from wishing to ingratiate himself with the new Queen, Sir John had reason to resent the Duke who had had him imprisoned in 1552. Also, the Duke's brother had recently been awarded lands previously granted to Sir John, and had taken first place as one of the two MPs for Oxfordshire after the elections of March 1553.

By 15 July, news had reached London that Sir John and another gentleman had assembled a force of over 6,000 men and cavalry to support Mary who was in residence in Kenninghall Castle in Norfolk.*

Even though the rumour of such an armed force must have undermined the Council's support for Queen Jane in London, Mary herself clearly feared the intentions of Sir John and, on 22 July she ordered him to disband his troops. On 25 July (or maybe even earlier), he proclaimed Mary as Queen, at Oxford and on 29 July, he was reported as accompanying the Princess Elizabeth into London, she, "all in green, gardyed with whytt velvet saten taffety".

Mary's accession was popular and, having quickly asserted her authority over the country, she began to reward her supporters. In January 1554, when the Court of Augmentations was disbanded, Sir John, as its Treasurer, was granted an annuity of £300 a year as financial compensation and, on 15 March he was presented with a chain worth 200 crowns (4 crowns = £1) as a token of the Queen's special esteem. The ultimate honour was awarded in April when the House of Lords' Journal records Sir John as having been ennobled as Baron Williams of Thame. He was also given the office of Lord

---

* 6,000 soldiers seems an exaggerated figure in view of the practicalities – organisation and supplies.

Chamberlain to the prince of Spain which leads us on to the next and perhaps most controversial aspect of Mary's reign.

The new queen was deeply attached to her Spanish roots. She could even speak the language. In order to secure her own position and the restoration of the Catholic faith, she quickly drew up a marriage treaty between herself and Prince Philip. This determination resulted in a marriage at Winchester Cathedral in the summer of 1554. All this, in spite of wholesale opposition from her own supporters as well as from English Protestants – an opposition which more than any other single factor, explains Mary's failure to win back England to Catholicism.

Lord Williams formally met Prince Philip[*] at Southampton on 20 July 1554, having first escorted him up the Channel with a fleet of 150 English ships to ensure the Prince's safety against any treacherous attempt by the French to prevent the marriage. Once Philip had joined the Queen, his unpopularity and that of the Spanish courtiers around him caused the royal couple, accompanied by Lord Williams and other attendants, to retreat from London to Richmond Palace for a while; such were the fears for their safety.

In July 1554, as the recently created Lord Chamberlain of Philip's household, Lord Williams was granted a pension of 1,000 crowns by the new King of England, a title granted to Philip by the terms of the marriage treaty. At about the same time, a letter from the Imperial Ambassador to Charles V,

---

[*] Recently created King of Naples for the sake of his status by his father, Emperor Charles V.

describes how Lord Williams was standing by the Queen when she received a humble apology from one of Williams's enemies for his hostile attitude to Williams and other courtiers.

Philip only resided in England for nineteen months – he disliked his wife, his position in England, the insularity of the English Court and the constant friction between the Spanish and English courtiers. In 1556, he became King of Spain when his father abdicated, and once he left England in July 1557, following a final three month visit, he never saw his wife again. She went through a series of hysterical false pregnancies. Her swollen body was a symptom of the illness which contributed to her relatively early death on 17 November 1558, aged 38.

During these four tumultuous years, Lord Williams was responsible for the smooth running of the King's household whether he was in residence or not, and for this, he received a salary of £100 a year. However, a letter written in 1558 by the Spanish Ambassador to King Philip says that Williams is owed £400 in salary payments and a further £40 granted to him for a velvet cloak or cape which was clearly a personal gift and therefore much esteemed. No authorisation for payment was forthcoming, so a later, rather plaintive letter from a new Ambassador to Philip, written on 18 April 1559, says that Williams "has gone to the Queen (Elizabeth) to complain of your Majesty and of me for not paying for his service".

On 8 May 1559, Philip, still resident in Flanders and reluctant to take up his responsibilities in Spain, replied as follows to the Ambassador: "You will order the Chamberlain to be paid all that is owing to his wages and, for the sable cloak which he claims to receive every year, you will pay him £30 for each one he should have received which was the arrangement made with him". In a postscript written in Philip's own hand, he says, "Do not give him any more. For any good he is at present, I do not see any reason for giving him a pension or anything else". Thus ended what seems to have been little more than a businesslike relationship between the King and a rather irritating English servant.

Interesting as the personal relationship between Lord Williams and the royal couple may have been, it is Williams's involvement with the religious and political developments of Mary's reign which should most define our opinion of the man at that time.

The Queen had to rely on a loyal gentry and aristocratic class to ensure the success of her policies, the chief of which was to restore Papal authority in England. We are not able to ascertain how far English people had taken to the new Protestant form of religion after centuries of loyalty to the old religion. Catholicism had offered them the prospect of a good life after death, provided the absolute authority of the Roman Church and its rules were accepted. Among these were the observance of Saints' days, attendance at the Latin Mass, confession and prayers for the repose of the souls of the dead. Such teachings were virulently denounced by the Protestants whose most prominent spokesman in the 1540s and up to 1553 was Thomas Cranmer, Archbishop of Canterbury.

He had sanctioned King Henry's annulment[*] of his marriage with Mary's mother; he had also brought in two Protestant Prayer Books in the English language and had ordered the English Bible to be read in all church services. He had also ordered the destruction of the chantries where prayers for the souls of dead relatives were said; the destruction of church ornaments and the replacement of altars, where the sacrifice of the body and blood of Christ was re-enacted, by tables where a meal of bread and wine was to be taken in memory of the Last Supper of Christ on Earth.

The Queen's hatred of all that Cranmer had brought about was soon translated into action when she ordered his arrest, trial and, in spite of his recantation, his execution by burning.

---

[*] An annulment is an assertion that a marriage has never in fact been legitimate and is therefore not the same as a divorce whereby a marriage is actually ended.

CHAPTER VII
THE BURNING OF THE BISHOPS

It was in his capacity as High Steward of Oxford and not as Sheriff, that Williams actually supervised the execution of Cranmer and Bishops Ridley and Latimer. The office had been deliberately revived by the Queen so as to infiltrate local government with officers whom she knew to be loyal to her in the vital matter of re-imposing the Roman Catholic Church in England.

However, Williams was acting as Sheriff of Oxford when he took charge of the three bishops at Brentford on 8 March 1554 and brought them to Oxford to await trial. In April, they were lodged in the Bocardo Prison opposite St Michael's Church in Corn Market where they stayed until, on a sunny 16 October 1555, Ridley and Latimer[*] were brought out to suffer their execution. A contemporary illustration shows Cranmer blessing them from an upper window as the two men made their way to the place of execution in a shallow ditch outside Balliol College, where today a

---

[*] Latimer had himself presided over the burning of a Catholic priest in 1538.

cross is marked in the road. It must have been a very tense and noisy event because the authorities feared "any tumult that might aryse" and, in an engraving in Foxe's "Book of Martyrs" which depicts the event, there are twenty-three pikes to be seen – presumably ready for use should the crowd cause any disruption of the proceedings.

When the two bishops had been obliged to listen to a sermon by a Catholic priest, they knelt down before Lord Williams and other officials and Ridley asked if he could speak, "but two or three words". Williams consulted the Mayor and the Vice-Chancellor of the University, but the latter "ran hastily up to him" (Ridley) and "stopped his mouth", refusing to let him speak unless he recanted. Then, "Master Ridley gave some napkins to Lord Williams's gentlemen, and some nutmegs and roots of ginger, his Diall" (watch), "and other personal possessions to those who stood around him". He then asked Lord Williams if he would act as a messenger to the Queen on his behalf to ensure that several poor men and his sister be cared for in the future. He went on to say his brother held the actual request which he would give to Williams later and that God would reward him for carrying out the request. Latimer, who was probably too fragile and terrified to speak (he was in his 70th year), was then bound to the stake with Ridley, the faggots (money had been paid to the executioner to ensure they were dry and would therefore burn fiercely) were heaped up against them and the fire was applied.

A graphic illustration of the burning of the two men appears in the "Book of Martyrs" with Lord Williams, labelled, sitting in an armchair witnessing the event.

Incidentally, the city records of Oxford include items in the accounts of this occasion:

"For wine to my Lord and his retinue at the burning of the Bishops, 3 shillings 4 pence".

"For two pairs of gloves double-garnished for my Lady Williams, 4 shillings". (Were they Woodstock gloves?)

The following March, the Queen sent for Williams to instruct him to supervise the execution at Oxford of Thomas Cranmer, former Archbishop of Canterbury.

At 9 o'clock on the morning of 21 March 1556, "a foul and rainy day", Williams entered the city with "a great traine of waiting men lest Cranmer's death should raise any tumult" and went straight to St Mary's Church in the High Street. Cranmer[*] was then brought into the church and during the sermon given by a priest, Cranmer was seen to be "weeping copiously". He then began to deliver a last sermon from the pulpit, but when he began to denounce the Pope, Lord Williams stopped him saying, "Play the Christian man, remember your recantations and do not dissemble". "Alas, my Lord", said Cranmer, "I have been a man that all my life loved plainness and never dissembled till now against the truth which I am most sorry for".

Cranmer, whose distress was made worse by his having signed seven recantations (denials) of his Protestant faith, was thus retracting them and later that day, he was to place the hand that had signed those papers into the flames to burn first.

---

[*] His last meal included stewed prunes which "ensured the prisoner would not suffer from a bad digestion in view of the difficulties he was about to face"!

Lord Williams then accompanied Cranmer to the stake. Pollard in his book, "Thomas Cranmer and the English Reformation", writes that Cranmer "walked quickly through Brasenose Lane out of the gate by St Michael's to the spot designated in front of Balliol College. He was now bald, having been shaved at his degradation, and with a white beard nearly to his waist. He was bound by a steel band to the stake. There were 150 faggots of furze and 100 faggots of wood. The Venetian Ambassador said he threw a recantation into the flames as he was being tied to the stake". When an argument broke out between Cranmer and a Catholic cleric from Brasenose College, Williams is said by a later chronicler to have cried out, "Make short, make short!", but to whom the remark was directed is not made clear.

Then, one of two Spanish friars ran up to Lord Williams, saying that the Archbishop was all mixed up in his mind and would die in great desperation. It is at this stage, in Foxe's account, that an interesting interpretation creeps in. Foxe implies that Williams knew that Cranmer was at last at peace with his conscience and therefore he only smiled at the friar and kept silent. Why would Williams, whose career rise was linked to the interests of Queen Mary, be portrayed as having allowed Cranmer freedom from further argument with the Spanish friar? Is it perhaps because Foxe published his works when Williams was still remembered favourably at Court, and particularly by Queen Elizabeth herself? Also, Williams's family had connections with many important families who would not wish to be associated with a man who could be said to have been a willing servant of the government in what was the single most traumatic domestic event in Mary's reign.

Lord Williams presides over the burning of the two bishops

Lord Williams presides over the burning of Thomas Cranmer

CHAPTER VIII
LORD WILLIAMS'S WEALTH

Although several details of the sources of Lord Williams's income have already been cited elsewhere, they are brought together here to give the reader a more coherent impression of the wealth he accumulated. To get a rough equivalent in contemporary terms, one should multiply sums by 500; even so, values then were very different from ours today e.g. oil did not exist then and wool and salt were staple commodities.

In Williams's time, the holding of a Crown office not only gave the holder much valued status and influence but it was also a vital source of revenue. Such income came from the salary granted by the office itself and from the fees paid by those who approached the office holder in his capacity as a patron, for the purchase of lesser offices or favours.

An indication of how Williams built up his wealth can be ascertained from a list of various payments he received for his offices at Court. He was paid £10 p.a. for keeping the King's greyhound, £50 p.a. as Master of the King's Jewels and then £320 p.a. for the Treasurership of the Court of Augmentations which became an annuity when he was obliged to give up that post in 1554. As Lord Chamberlain to King Philip, he received £100 p.a. and when he became President of the Council of Wales, he was granted a salary of £1,000.

Not only did Williams hold those lucrative offices listed above but he held a host of minor sinecures which added both to his income and to his influence. He frequently received grants of land from the Crown instead of payments for work done; he became the Steward of various estates, including the Manor of Notley and the lands of the Bishop of Oxford, taking from them whatever sums he considered his due. He was made Master of the King's Cygnets on the Thames and Keeper of the King's Swans in all the waters of England outside the Duchy of Lancaster, which again brought him fees.

The setting up of a family network was an important ambition for all land-owning families and this was true of Lord Williams. First, he exploited his distant family links with Thomas Cromwell to enter the Court and, in 1524 he married Elizabeth Bledlowe, a rich widow who brought land and property to the marriage. His second marriage was to Margaret Wentworth, the daughter of Sir Thomas Wentworth who was later to be ennobled. Her grandmother on her mother's side was Anne Stonor, and thus the Stonor properties were eventually joined with those of the Williams family. His two daughters both married into well-endowed families and incidentally, his siblings also profited from their relationship to their brother.

To further augment this already considerable wealth, he received gifts from his royal patrons. In March 1554, Queen Mary made him a gift of a silver chain worth 200 crowns when only four other Courtiers received such a valuable New Year gift. At Christmas 1555, the Queen gave him a silver cup weighing 38½ ounces when only six other courtiers, including Princess Elizabeth, Anne of Cleves (still alive!), the two Archbishops and two other noblemen received more valuable gifts.

The annual rents he collected from the former monastic lands of Thame Abbey amounted to £84. 6s. 8d. The references in 1548 to lands from which he was receiving rent by virtue of having purchased licences from the Crown to collect such rents, are too numerous to list here.

He bought a large house in London which was next to the Spanish Embassy. He had already bought Rycote, a sumptuous house, from the son of a former treasurer to both Henry VII and Henry VIII. It was a house worthy to receive the Privy Council in August 1540 when Henry VIII was enjoying his honeymoon with his 5th wife, Catherine Howard – later to be executed! He also entertained Princess Elizabeth at Rycote in May 1554 and in April 1555.

At the end of his life Lord Williams held the Lordship of Thame, the manors of Rycote, Charlford, Albury, Weston-on-the-Green, Stokenchurch, Beaconsfield, Notley, Crendon, Brill, North and South Hinksey, Oddington, Chesterton, Wendlebury, Lewknor, Sunningwell, Chislehampton, Horton, Beckley, Wytham and four others elsewhere. All but three properties, Rycote, Burghfield and Comber in Wales, were acquired as spoils of the Church.

His epitaph on his tomb refers to his wealth saying (in Latin), "As a man of merit and through his office, he was able to acquire the wealth of money and as a good man, behold, he made use of it". Such a comment sits comfortably with that of Pope Alexander VI (1492 – 1503) who said, "Since God has given us the Papacy, let us use it to our advantage".

View of Rycote House

CHAPTER IX
THE FINAL YEAR

When the newly proclaimed Queen Elizabeth rode from Hatfield into London in November 1558, she was accompanied by 32 favoured Lords, among whom was Lord Williams. Doubtless there were two lines of thought passing through his mind as he rode in the procession; would the former Lady Elizabeth take into account his daring support and the hospitality he had offered her in the dark days of Queen Mary's reign and reward him? Or would Queen Elizabeth, with her Protestant inclinations and her desire to reconcile the nation, decide to punish the man whose political and religious loyalties were plainly so fickle? Her decision, taken among dozens of others in the hectic early weeks of her reign, was neither to reward nor to punish in the way Williams might have expected.

For his loyalty to her and for his administrative experience, the Queen appointed him, in February 1559, to the Presidency of the governing Council of Wales, his father's native country. Thus, the Queen's wariness of him may account for her steering him well clear of the centre of power and into what had become a backwater of English political life, where he could only enjoy local political power and patronage, and very little, if any, national influence.

By the time of his appointment, the Queen must have known his health was failing fast. Indeed, his move to Ludlow Castle, the seat of government of Wales, was delayed until June 1559 when he felt well enough to make the journey. For the next four months, the records show that he carried out his presidential duties as conscientiously as any other Tudor official in poor health. In his capacity as Lord Lieutenant of Wales, he even sent 700 soldiers to Berwick to defend that city against possible attacks from Scotland.

Lord Williams died on 14 October 1559 and while suitable preparations were being made for the transport of his embalmed body to Thame where he was to be interred, he lay in the Castle Chapel at Ludlow. His funeral was finally conducted at 8 o'clock on the morning of 15 November at St Mary's Church, Thame. The church walls were covered with 120 black hangings. The body was accompanied into the church by three Heralds of Arms, a great banner bearing his heraldic arms, eight other great standards, twelve dozen heraldic shields and 100 mourners. The service was conducted according to the newly re-introduced Protestant rites with a sermon and the Communion was distributed from a table and not from the altar. After the ceremony, a large sum of money and nine gowns were distributed among the poorest people of Thame.

When the embalmed body had been lowered into its final resting place in the centre of the church, a highly elaborate, carved effigy of Lord Williams was laid over it. There it remained until some of

Oliver Cromwell's soldiers who stabled their horses in the church during the Civil War, were said to have dug up the corpse and used it for target practice! When the stone effigy was later put back in place, the head was pointing towards the East instead of the feet, which was the norm. At a time when the inhabitants of Thame had reason to hate their erstwhile lord, the presumed mistake may have been a deliberate insult to a man no longer able to fend for himself!

In March 1559, Williams, "being sick of body but of sound mind", had made his will. By that time, Queen Elizabeth's religious leanings towards Protestantism had become apparent and so it was in character that the form of words he used in his will did not betray any lingering attachment to Catholicism. Indeed, there is one interesting incident which may indicate a genuine Protestant conviction at last; he sent for a returned protestant exile, John Jewel, later to be Bishop of Sarum (Salisbury), when he was sick and had him stay with him at Ludlow Castle in the summer of 1559.

Nevertheless, the all too human tendency among the uncommitted to finally hedge their bets and even to repent their sins, comes through in the provisions made in his will for the distribution of his estate. He left the revenues of the rectories and parsonages of Brill, Oakley and Borstall for the building of a grammar school with a master and an usher (assistant school master) to be built by the church where it still stands today and with his arms carved over the entrance. He also left money for almshouses to care for five poor men and one poor woman (note the sexist bias!) from Thame. Lee in his "History of Thame Church", 1883, makes the interesting observation, "Did he begin to realise the increasing evils which the changes had brought about – the decay of religion, the selfishness, the need for educational institutions, the sufferings of the poor – and thus he resolved to make some atonement, or did he see in his two sons' deaths, some sign of divine disapproval, fear of which had been instilled in him when he was young and which he could never quite put out of his mind?" To his wife, as well as several manors and his London house at Elsingspital, he left various bowls and flagons, each with its weight carefully noted down. He also bequeathed to her two gilded salt cellars, a cup with a gilded cover given by Princess Mary at the christening of one of his children, along with items given by the Duchess of Norfolk, the Earl of Bedford and a New Year's gift of a cup from Princess Elizabeth. Various other goblets, silver dishes, salt cellars, jugs and spoons as well as more ordinary pots and ceramic bowls were also left to his widow.

Each of his daughters married; Isabella to Sir Richard Wenman whose family lived on at Thame Park until the mid-twentieth century and after whom the school in Towersey Lane was originally named. Marjery, Queen Elizabeth's favourite and named by her, "My Black Crow" (either after her father's coat of arms or because of her dark complexion), married first Sir Henry, later Lord Henry Norreys, then Lord Thomas Wentworth and still later she took two other husbands! No male heir survived, so the title and the right to the coat of arms disappeared with our subject's death.

School Statutes 1575 and John Williams's signature.

CHAPTER X
ASSESSMENT OF THE LIFE OF JOHN WILLIAMS

John Williams has attracted comment, much of it hostile, over the centuries and although I leave it to the reader to decide what to think, it is interesting to learn what others have said about him.

The earliest report on Williams occurs in October 1551 when the Imperial Ambassador writes to the Emperor Charles V that the people loathe Williams and that the government uses this unpopularity to curry favour by arresting and imprisoning him.

In March 1555, the next Imperial Ambassador reported that Williams was treacherous and that he was devoted to Princess Elizabeth. This was only a year after Williams had been ennobled; seven months before the burning of the bishops and written while Philip of Spain was still in residence and remained so until August. For Williams thus to ingratiate himself with Princess Elizabeth when his position was so insecure and thus to defy the government was either very reckless or very brave. At that time, there were still strong expectations that the Queen could have a baby – indeed, an announcement was made on 4 May 1555 to this effect, only two months after the Ambassador's report – and the birth of an heir would have seriously threatened the chances of Elizabeth ever becoming queen.

In Elizabeth's reign, Foxe's "Book of Martyrs" refrains from criticising the man who supervised the burning of the three bishops. Foxe knew better than to alienate a favourite of the Queen, whose daughters had married well. Thus, Williams escaped criticism in a book which, besides the Bible, was the most commonly found work in literate Elizabethan households.

J. Dunkin in his "History and Antiquities of the Hundreds of Bullington and Ploughley" (London, 1823), offered a seemingly contradictory assessment of Williams. He wrote, "This person was deeply engaged in the criminal transactions of that eventful period and made a distinguished figure in the reigns of Edward VI and Mary". Such comment leaves the reader wondering how he could be both guilty of criminal offences and yet be a "distinguished figure" in each of two very different reigns.

In 1883, F.G. Lee in his "History of St Mary's Church" (London, 1883), makes the most considered, yet sarcastic statement on the career of Williams: "The wit and wisdom, discretion and foresight displayed by the influential knight of Rycote in taking care to be walking on the sunshiny side of the street ... will no doubt be appreciated by all those enlightened and benevolent persons who look upon self-seeking and selfishness as natural virtues". Later, he writes, "As a subservient courtier, an obsequious follower and faithful servant, he was probably without equal".

Nevertheless, he concludes, "He must have been possessed of considerable abilities, clear-headedness, caution, shrewdness, art and discretion", and with this final judgement even his most virulent detractors would have to agree.

N.J. O'Conor in his "Godes Peace and the Queenes" (London, 1934), wrote, "He was not a man of an original mind but a man who would efficiently carry out the orders of his superiors". This seems a less than accurate judgement on a man who set out to accumulate so much personal wealth that he was summoned before the Council on four occasions (1552, 1553, 1556 and 1558) to account for his activities, who raised troops for Mary Tudor before it was clear that the Duke of Northumberland's plans for Queen Jane would not succeed and who kept up links with Princess Elizabeth in seeming defiance of the prevailing government attitude towards her. Finally, Williams's admission of having been "negligent and careless" at the court of Augmentations hardly justifies the claim that he worked efficiently for his superiors.

Then in 1935, two former teachers at Lord Williams's School, J.H. Brown and W. Guest published "The History of Thame School". They plainly saw the founder as a man of "integrity" which, in the light of the evidence, hardly stands up to examination. They also said, "A man of less worth could hardly have survived the troubles of the time", but much depends on our interpretation of the word "worth"!

So what judgement can we pass on Lord Williams in the twenty-first century? It is clear that his loyalties, like those of the Vicar of Bray, were firm until he decided to change his mind! He had the persistence, energy and foresight to accumulate a vast fortune and the social status to go with it. He never revealed any strong religious convictions, moving from the old faith to the reformed as those in power directed. No doubt, successive governments had little choice but to use turncoats such as Williams because no one who remained steadfast in any particular belief could stay near the centre of power and survive in the mid-Tudor period. After all, Williams became a very experienced mover in the ways of government but was never in a position to pose a threat to the monarch.

All we can do, to judge him fairly, is to see him as he was seen by the people of the time – a useful official to the Crown, an object of jealousy to the upper classes and a landlord loathed by his tenants. He was corrupt even in the eyes of the Tudor Court, yet he must have had a certain personal ability to win the trust of Queen Mary and the cautious affection of Queen Elizabeth.

Perhaps the last word on our subject should lie with John Hussey's "Rycote" in Country Life, Vol. 63 (1), (London, 1928). When describing Williams's tomb in Thame Church, he noted that his head is facing the altar rather than his feet and he writes that this is, "the only occasion in which he appears to be facing the wrong way"!

Lord Williams and his first wife, Elizabeth Bledlowe,
St Mary's Church, Thame
(Photograph, Philip Mallon, 2008)

DATE LIST

1500

Born in Burghfield, Berkshire, second son of John Williams from Glamorgan.

1524

July   Married Elizabeth Bledlowe, a rich widow – three sons predeceased him without children; two daughters survived him. Isabella inherited Thame Park, married Sir Richard Wenman (family lived in the area until 20th century). Marjery married Sir Henry Norreys, son of the alleged lover of Anne Boleyn who always denied the relationship, much to Queen Elizabeth's relief.

1526

Williams was a Chancery official at Hampton Court for Cardinal Wolsey, Henry VIII's principal minister.

1527

Granted £10 for keeping a greyhound for the King.

1530

6 April — Appointed Clerk of the King's Jewels; salary: 20 marks (nearly £14 = £7,000 now)

Summer — Henry VIII rode through Thame with Anne Boleyn at his side and Queen Catherine (of Aragon) riding behind.

1531

6 March — Received some lands of the executed 3rd Duke of Buckingham.

1535

Williams made Justice of the Peace for Oxford, Oxfordshire and Buckinghamshire

Accepted a commission from Thomas Cromwell to enquire into the state of the monasteries and their lands in Oxfordshire.

He entertained Thomas Cromwell's son, Gregory.

1536

April — Joint Master of the King's Jewels with Thomas Cromwell.

Oct. 27	Took action against the Lincolnshire rebels. Wrote to T. Cromwell concerning local landlords, "I have never seen such a sight of asses so unlike gentlemen".

1537

	Still a J.P., enquiring into the monasteries and Joint Master of the Crown Jewels.
Oct. 15	Present at christening of Prince Edward, Henry's only surviving legitimate son and whose mother, Jane Seymour, died after his birth.
Oct. 18	He was knighted – Sir John Williams.

1538

	He probably bought the Renaissance country house at Rycote.
Mar. 7-11	Supervising the stripping of all the valuables of Abingdon Abbey.
May 2	Refused to sell gold cramp rings from the Crown Jewels to a citizen because the King was holding all the gold.
May 8	The citizen received his gold cramp rings – had he bribed Williams?
Sept. 21	He wrote to Thomas Cromwell describing how the shrine and the high altar at Winchester had been dismantled.

| Dec. 24 | 7 pm – a big fire occurred at Williams's London house at Elsingspital (bought for £530) during which many of the royal jewels disappeared! |

1539

Rycote estate was enclosed to keep out commoners and to keep in his deer and sheep.

Aug. 31	He inspected Studley Priory where his sister was prioress and found no evidence of wrong doing.
Sept. 20	He was officially styled a knight for the first time.
Nov./Dec.	He was supervising the closure of religious houses in the Thame area including Thame and Notley Abbeys.

1540

Jan. 3	He was at Blackheath when the King met Anne of Cleves, his 4th wife.
Jan. 6	He probably attended the ensuing marriage.
Jun.	After the fall of Thomas Cromwell, he became sole Master of the King's Jewels.
Aug. 26	The Privy Council met at Rycote where Henry VIII was on his 5th honeymoon.
Sept.	He became chief tax collector for Oxfordshire.

1541

He was elected MP for Oxfordshire until 1544.

During the summer, Henry again passed through Thame.

1542

He was accepting grants of land, leasing some of it out and making huge profits.

Mar. 15　He was granted Thame Abbey and some abbey land by the Crown – annual rent value £84 6s 8d.

He was made Keeper of all the royal swans in England outside the Duchy of Lancaster and Master of the royal cygnets on the Thames.

He became Steward of all the cathedral lands of the newly created diocese of Oxford.

He was granted the Manor and gardens of Notley.

Sept.　Thame Abbey lands were taken from him and granted to the Diocese of Oxford but were re-granted to him in 1547.

1543

May 6　He was commissioned to supervise the sale of all ex-monastic land that the Crown decided to dispose of.

1544

Mar. 31　He exchanged the office of Master of the King's Jewels out of which he had made £16,667 for himself, and

	took on the office of Treasurer of the Court of Augmentations at a salary of £320 p.a.
May 22	He was granted a licence to retain 10 men in livery (a private force carrying much status). He became captain of 20 archers and 40 pikemen from Oxfordshire.
Sept. 10	He was made Master Forester of Whittlewood Forest in Northamptonshire.

1545

He became Commissioner of Benevolences whose duty it was to extract forced loans and gifts from rich subjects.

1546

He became Commissioner for the Chantries – where masses had been sung for the repose of the souls of the dead – in Northamptonshire, Oxfordshire and Rutland. His job was to assess the value to the Crown of those chantries, free chapels and colleges.

1547

28 Jan	When Henry VIII died, a survey of the Royal Jewels was made. Suspicions were voiced that Williams may have been helping himself to some items between 1540

	and 1544.
Jul. 8	The Crown granted some land already granted to Sir John, to the Duke of Somerset.
Oct.	He was elected MP for Oxfordshire again.
Nov.	As Commissioner to the Navy, his job was to see how many ships were sea-worthy.

1548

He continued as MP for Oxfordshire, Commissioner for the Chantries, the Navy and was still Treasurer of the Court of Augmentations.

1549

Feb. 15	He began making an inventory of all church goods in England.
Jun. 9	The first Book of Common Prayer was issued.
Jul. 19	He was putting down riots in Oxfordshire against the Book of Common Prayer. The rebels attacked Thame Park and Rycote Park.
Aug. 7	Williams informed the Council that the papist rebels had been punished.
Oct. 10	As one of 3 commissioners, he arrested the Duke of Somerset at Windsor. Manor of Thame returned to Williams from Somerset's control.

1550

He bought the old hospital of the Thame Guild of St Christopher and replaced it by a new row of almshouses near the church, which still exists. A priest was to be paid £6 p.a. and there was to be a chaplain to help the vicar. He put out £10 13s 9d to support 6 paupers in Thame.

1551

Aug. 20	His son, Henry, married to the daughter of Baron Stafford, died without heirs.
Oct. 26	Williams was arrested on the orders of the Council.

1552

Apr. 3	He appeared before the Privy Council, charged with having paid out pensions to ex- monks without authorisation when the royal coffers were nearly empty.
Apr. 8	He was put in solitary confinement in the Fleet Prison.
Apr. 25	He was allowed to walk in the garden and received visits from his family
May 22	He was released on the grounds of ill health.
Jun. 2	He was granted full liberty.

1553

Mar.	He was elected MP for Oxfordshire but yielded the first of the 2 seats to the Duke of Northumberland's brother.
Jul. 6	Edward VI died. Williams left London for Oxfordshire.
Jul. 13	He proclaimed Mary as Queen.
Jul 15	He is said to have raised 6,000 troops to send to Northampton to aid Mary's claim.
Jul. 22	Mary ordered him to disband his troops – too dangerous a threat to her.
Jul. 25	Williams proclaimed Mary in Oxford city.
Jul. 29	He met Princess Elizabeth for the first time and escorted her to London.
Dec. 17	He was ordered to appear before the Council with a full explanation of his financial transactions at the Court of Augmentations.

1554

Jan 22	The Court of Augmentations was disbanded. Williams received £320.
Mar. 8	As Sheriff of Oxfordshire, he took charge of the 3 bishops at Brentford.
Mar. 15	Mary gave him a silver chain worth 200 crowns.
Apr. 3	Williams received oaths of loyalty to Prince Philip from his servants and officers.
Apr. 5-8	The process of ennoblement as Baron Williams of

	Thame occurred and he was made Lord Chamberlain to Philip's household.
Apr. 12	Williams is at sea escorting Philip's ships to England. At about this time, he was made High Steward of Oxford, a new office with powers direct from the Crown and by-passing all other city officials.
May 20	He took charge of Princess Elizabeth at Richmond and entertained her at Rycote on her way to confinement at Woodstock.
Jul. 20	Williams met Philip at Southampton. Philip granted pensions of 1,000 crowns to Williams and 7 other officials.
Sept. 3	Queen Mary had Williams at her side when she received the apologies of a nobleman for offending Williams.

1555

Mar. 27	He visited Princess Elizabeth without permission.
Apr.	She stayed at Rycote en route for London.
Summer	He paid back £644. 19s to the accounts of the Court of Augmentations as part of the debt he owed the Court.
Oct. 16	He supervised the burning of Bishop Latimer of Worcester (70) and of Bishop Ridley of London (55).
Dec. 25	Queen Mary gave Williams a silver cup weighing 38 ½ oz. Only 6 courtiers including Princess Elizabeth, the ex-queen, Anne of Cleves, and the 2 archbishops

received more valuable gifts.

1556

Mar. 9	The Queen commanded Williams to organise the burning of Thomas Cranmer.
Mar. 21	Cranmer was burnt outside Balliol College, Oxford.
Jun. 5	Williams appeared before the Council to explain a debt of £2,500 he owed the to the Crown.
Jun. 10	He was pardoned and released.
Oct. 26	His wife Elizabeth died and was buried at Rycote.

1557

Apr. 19	He married Margaret, daughter of the first Baron Wentworth of Nettlestead, Suffolk, whose brother surrendered Calais to the French.

1558

May	He appeared before the Council to show his 1556 pardon and to pay back debts.
Nov. 24	Princess Elizabeth became Queen Elizabeth I. He was one of 32 Lords who accompanied her into London.

1559

Feb.	He was appointed Lord President of the Council for Wales and the Marches and Lord Lieutenant for Wales with a salary of £1,000 a year.
	Illness prevented him travelling to Ludlow Castle to take up his duties.
Feb 18	His unmarried eldest son, John, died in London.
Mar. 8	Williams made his will – already standardised in Protestant form.
May 8	King Philip II of Spain gave instructions that Williams be paid sums due.
Jun.	Williams arrived at Ludlow.
Sept. 25	The Queen ordered him to raise 700 troops to send up to fortify the defences of Berwick Castle.
Oct 14	10 am Lord Williams died at Ludlow.
Nov. 15	8 am He was buried in Thame Church.

Printed in the United Kingdom
by Lightning Source UK Ltd.
134023UK00001B/259-312/P